SPECIAL DAYS

CLEAN UP AUSTRALIA DAY

JANE PFEIFFER

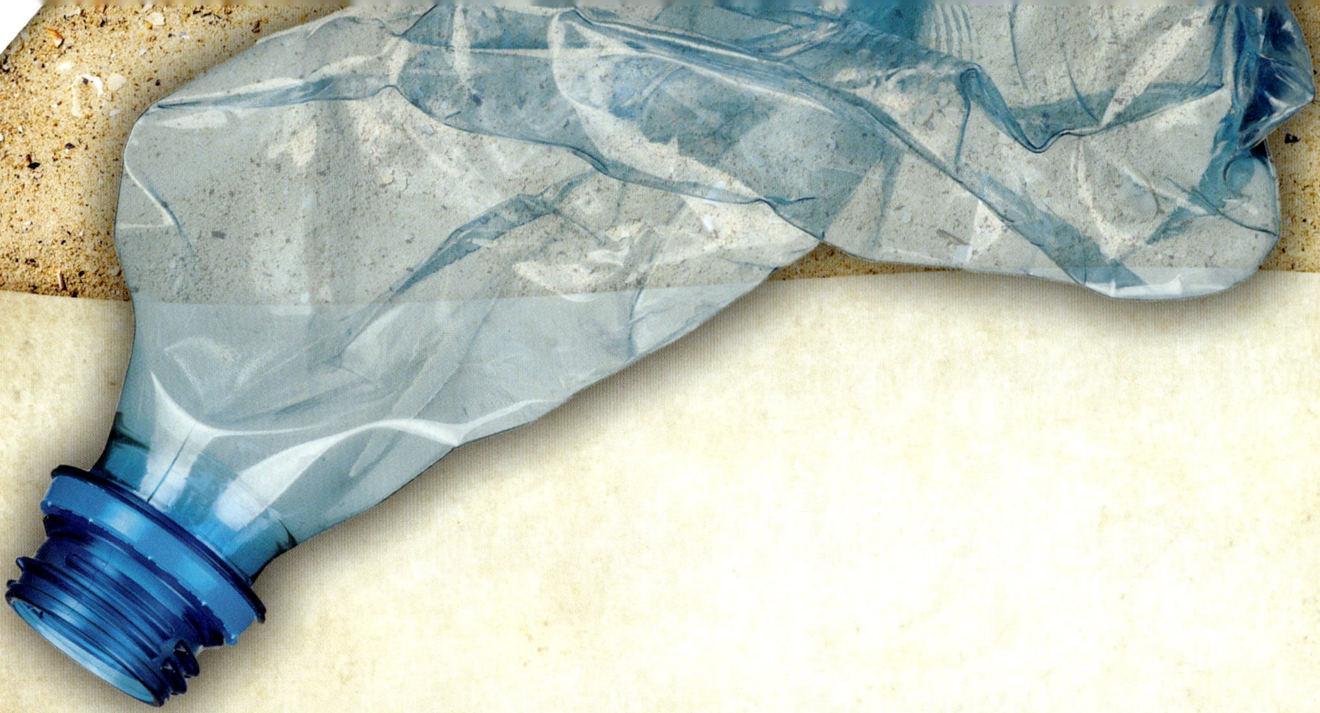

Redback Publishing
Suite 6, 13a Narabang Way,
Belrose NSW 2085
Australia

www.redbackpublishing.com
orders@redbackpublishing.com

ISBN 978-1-761401-59-6

Author: Jane Pfeiffer
Editor: Caroline Thomas
Design: Redback Publishing

Original illustrations © Redback Publishing 2025
Originated by Redback Publishing

Acknowledgements
Abbreviations: l—left, r—right, b—bottom, t—top, c—centre, m—middle
We would like to thank the following for permission to reproduce photographs: (Images © shutterstock, wikimediacommons)

p7br Edgloris Marys / Shutterstock.com
p12m rafapress / Shutterstock.com

A catalogue record for this book is available from the National Library of Australia

CONTENTS

SPECIAL DAYS

In Australia we celebrate or commemorate a number of special days throughout the year. Some are public holidays, which means that people can have the day off work or school. Some special days are marked with events and festivities.

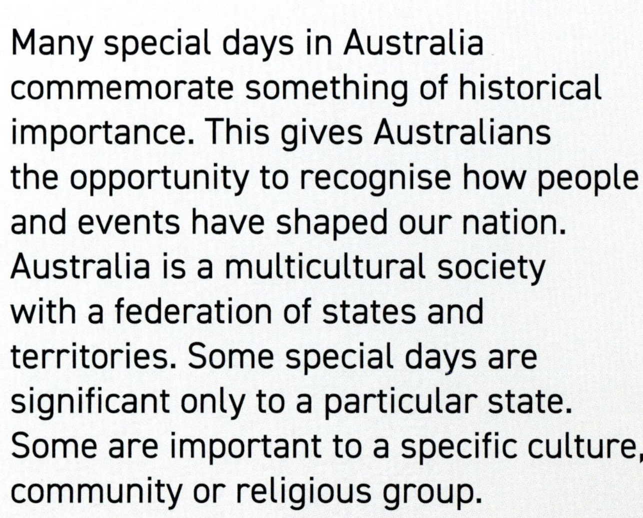

Many special days in Australia commemorate something of historical importance. This gives Australians the opportunity to recognise how people and events have shaped our nation. Australia is a multicultural society with a federation of states and territories. Some special days are significant only to a particular state. Some are important to a specific culture, community or religious group.

Special days are a chance to reflect on the past, to appreciate the world we know and to look to the future together. On these days, we celebrate some of the things that make Australia what it is today.

CLEAN UP AUSTRALIA DAY

Clean Up Australia is the non-profit organisation that introduced Clean Up Australia Day. Each year, community groups and charitable organisations encourage volunteers to use this special day to hold clean up events. Events include activities to clear litter from parks, rivers and beaches, and to encourage recycling.

DAY: Clean Up Australia Day
DATE: The first Sunday of March
WHERE: All states and territories
WHAT: National day when communities organise local events where people can volunteer to help clean up an area of their local environment

There are many Clean Up events held around the Nation, with thousands of people using the day to remove trash from their local areas and to forge stronger connections in their communities.

IAN KIERNAN AO

Ian Kiernan AO co-founded Clean Up Australia with Kim McKay. Kim was an entrepreneur and marketing consultant and Ian was an Australian yachtsman and a property developer. In 1987, while taking part in an around-the-world yacht race, Ian saw that the ocean was filled with rubbish.

When he returned home to Sydney in 1989, he organised a community event to help remove litter from the local parks and waterways. Ian named the event, Clean Up Sydney Harbour and used the day to raise awareness about how litter was being washed into the ocean. He inspired 40,000 people to volunteer and paved the way for the first official Clean Up Australia Day in 1990.

For his service to the Clean Up Australia campaign, the Clean up the World campaign and for inspiring and mobilising tens of millions of people around the globe, Ian Kiernan has received many awards, including:

- **1991** – awarded medal of the Order of Australia (OAM)
- **1994** – named Australian of the Year
- **1995** – awarded the Officer of the Order of Australia (AO)
- **1997/98** – named as one of Australia's National Living Treasures
- **1998** – awarded the Sasakawa Environment prize by the United Nations
- **1999** – World Citizenship Award
- **2001** – awarded the Centenary Medal

SCHOOLS CLEAN UP DAY

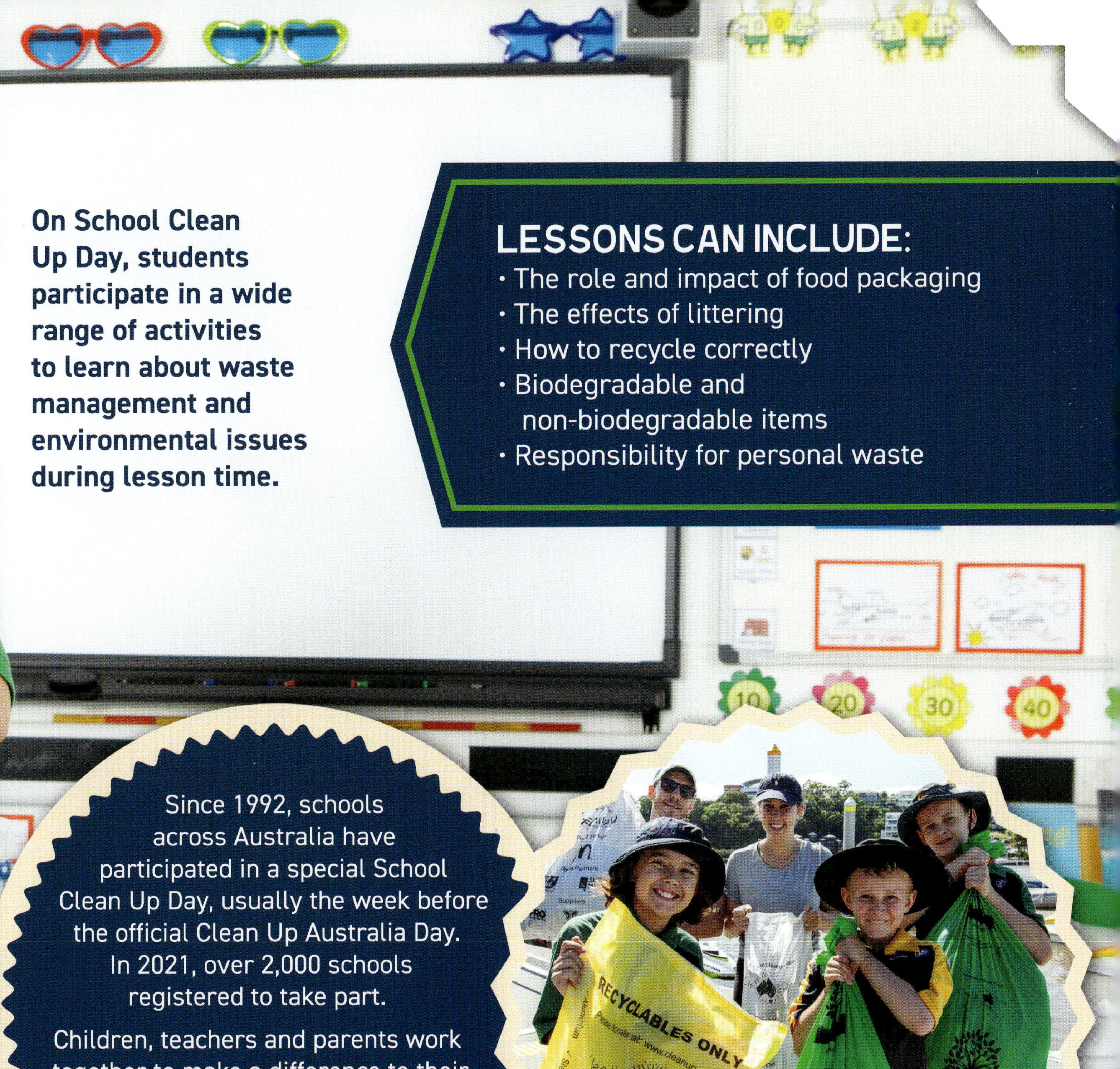

On School Clean Up Day, students participate in a wide range of activities to learn about waste management and environmental issues during lesson time.

LESSONS CAN INCLUDE:

- The role and impact of food packaging
- The effects of littering
- How to recycle correctly
- Biodegradable and non-biodegradable items
- Responsibility for personal waste

Since 1992, schools across Australia have participated in a special School Clean Up Day, usually the week before the official Clean Up Australia Day. In 2021, over 2,000 schools registered to take part.

Children, teachers and parents work together to make a difference to their school. Activities include picking up litter, cleaning classrooms and removing graffiti.

CLEAN UP THE WORLD

In 1993, Clean Up Day went international. Across 80 countries, more than 30 million people participated in a Clean Up the World Weekend. Today, Clean Up the World operates in partnership with the United Nations Environment Programme. It is one of the largest community-based environmental campaigns in the world with over 35 million volunteers across 133 countries.

Clean Up the World encourages communities all across the globe to come together to make a difference to their local environment. Volunteer groups work together and share experiences so that others can be inspired to take action and communities can benefit from a healthier environment.

THE GREAT NORTHERN CLEAN UP

The Great Northern Clean Up began in 2009, in response to differences north of the Tropic of Capricorn. The hotter climate, different tourist season as well as its eventful weather patterns mean that the perfect time for a Clean Up Day is much later in the year. The north of Australia observes The Great Northern Clean Up once the weather becomes cooler and the tourists have left, but before the monsoon and cyclone season can wash the rubbish into the ocean.

Over 1,100 northern locations now participate in the Great Northern Clean Up each year. Between August and October, thousands of volunteers remove rubbish from sites across northern Western Australia, the Northern Territory and Queensland.

CLEAN UP AUSTRALIA DAY EVENTS

All around Australia, businesses, schools and communities take the time to think about and organise Clean Up Australia Day events. Some events are large-scale, involving complex projects that include professional contractors as well as local businesses and community volunteers. Other events involve smaller community projects that can have a big impact on local environments. Any event, whether large or small, plays an important part in making Australia as environmentally healthy as it can be.

There are many ways to get involved in a Clean Up Australia Day event. Your local council will have a Clean Up Australia Day schedule that you can encourage your friends and family to join. Some youth groups such as scouts, guides and faith-based youth groups organise local Clean Up events, or you could rally your school to hold a Clean Up event. Sadly, litter is a year-round problem and organising a clean up group is a great idea at any time of year that best suits you and your group.

EQUIPMENT CHECKLIST

- Protective gloves
- Hat and sunscreen
- Closed shoes, like sneakers or boots
- Insect repellent
- Tools such as rakes and shovels
- Garbage bags
- Reusable water bottle to keep hydrated

EVERYDAY PREVENTION

REDUCE

Everyone can help to reduce the amount of rubbish that impacts our environment every day. The choices we make have a huge impact on our planet and there are simple things we can all do to help.

- Do NOT litter, instead encourage others to take their rubbish home
- Pick up any rubbish you see on the beach, in the bush or in parklands
- Say NO to single-use plastics, including bags, straws and balloons
- Don't buy new clothes that are unlikely to be worn more than once
- Don't buy poor quality or unnecessary household items
- Choose foods and products that have been grown or produced locally
- Plan your meals to prevent buying unnecessary food
- Don't overfill plates or lunchboxes

RE-USE

Australia is one of the most wasteful nations in the world. Furniture, clothing, electrical and household items all have the opportunity to be re-used, re-purposed or broken down into recyclable parts. The popularity of cheap products that are not intended to last for a long time has created a 'throw-away' culture. Cheap, fashionable products have become inexpensive and easily accessible but the environmental impact of this is devastating.

New items use massive amounts of water and carbon in their production and transportation, and the old products they replace are too often sent straight to landfill. Finding ways to re-use or re-purpose old items has a huge impact on the health of our planet. Always consider buying second-hand items before buying new items and choose new items that may be able to be sold or donated when they are no longer required.

RECYCLE

Huge amounts of the waste that is sent to landfill should instead be recycled. The production of new plastic, glass or aluminium uses more resources and produces a great deal more pollution than recycling existing materials.

LEARN THE COLOURED LID RECYCLING CODE:

- **Red** bin lid = LANDFILL
- **Blue** bin lid = Paper
- **Yellow** bin lid = plastics, glass, aluminium cans and steel lids

- Recycle soft plastics such as chip packets and bread bags in special collection bins at supermarkets
- Pack a litter free lunch, recycling or composting anything that isn't edible at home
- Buy clothes and household items at thrift shops, or swap with friends

COMPOSTING

Food scraps account for more than 40 percent of household rubbish in Australia. Every year, the average Australian household sends over $2,000 worth of groceries to landfill sites, to give off methane and carbon dioxide as they break down, contributing to global warming. Composting food scraps can significantly reduce the amount of waste going to landfill, while at the same time creating rich soil for our plants.

BACKYARD HELP

In households with a backyard, chickens and worms are two great ways to dispose of food scraps. Chickens have the added benefit of providing eggs in return for scraps and are one of the most effective (and natural) pest controllers. Chickens eat bugs that can attack garden plants and vegetable gardens. This adds protein to their eggs, while the bugs' exoskeletons provide calcium to harden chicken eggshells.

Worm farms are a great way to dispose of food scraps. The worms eat the scraps and excrete the remains as nutrient-rich soil. Worm farms have layers with filters so that any excess liquid can seep down into a special compartment, where it can be drained for use as a potent garden fertiliser.

LITTER

While volunteers continue to roll up their sleeves to clean up Australia's parks, beaches, waterways, roads and bushlands, the same amount of litter is being removed year after year.

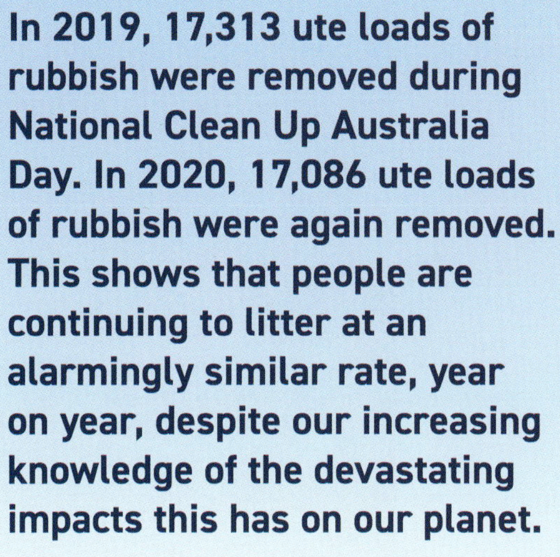

In 2019, 17,313 ute loads of rubbish were removed during National Clean Up Australia Day. In 2020, 17,086 ute loads of rubbish were again removed. This shows that people are continuing to litter at an alarmingly similar rate, year on year, despite our increasing knowledge of the devastating impacts this has on our planet.

ALL PLASTIC LITTER 2020

SOFT PLASTICS

FOOD PACKAGING

OTHER PLASTICS

Plastic waste actually increased by 5 percent from 2019 to 2020, with soft plastics, such as bags, making up almost 14 percent of all litter collected and over 40 percent of all plastics. Food packaging remains the most commonly littered item, making up almost 50 percent of all litter. Disappointingly, this amount is the same as it was the previous year, which points to two things: firstly, that food manufacturers continue to send foods to market that are too heavily packaged; secondly, that some consumers continue to ignore the damage that littering is causing to the planet.

POLLUTION

Litter is a common source of pollution in Australia. Most litter takes hundreds of years to break down, during which time it continues to pollute the environment. When it rains, litter dropped in the streets is often carried into stormwater drains that usually lead to nearby waterways.

Up to 12.7 million tonnes of plastic waste is washed into the world's oceans each year. There are now more than 46,000 pieces of plastic floating in every 2.5 square kilometres of the ocean. Ocean currents shift this dangerous pollution hundreds of kilometres from its original source to kill more than 1 million seabirds every year and more than 100,000 marine mammals.

CLIMATE CHANGE

In recent years, scientists have noticed that Earth's average temperature has been rising. This phenomenon is referred to as global warming. Scientists and many other people are very concerned that global warming will get much worse unless humans do something about it. Clean Up Australia helps to educate people about the impact that littering has on the planet and the strategies we can all use to bring about positive change.

In Australia, climate change means less rainfall, but rain that is more damaging when it does come. Increasingly severe bushfires are a natural consequence of changing weather patterns including excessively high temperatures for longer periods of time.

Household and industrial waste that goes to landfill generates 13 million tonnes of greenhouse gas emissions each year. Much of this waste is food that is left over from meals or that has gone bad before being eaten. While breaking down in landfill, food waste releases methane into the atmosphere. Clean Up Australia Day encourages people to think about what they throw away and to reconsider what should actually be discarded to landfill.

NATIVE ANIMALS

Over 50 percent of Australia's threatened species live in urban areas. Many species of birds, mammals, amphibians and reptiles live in cities and large towns, with many listed as under threat or endangered. Urban nature reserves, private gardens and backyards and even apartment balconies can be a safe haven for these native creatures.

Litter can encourage unwanted, invasive pests such as rats and foxes that often feed on littered food waste. They also bring disease and invade the habitats of native wildlife. Foxes are predators and will hunt and kill many different species of native animals, as well as small backyard pets such as chickens and rabbits.

INTO THE FUTURE

In the last 31 years, over 19 million people have volunteered their time on Clean Up Australia Day, spending over 38.5 million hours working toward the common goal of healing our planet. They found that about 80 percent of the trash removed could have been recycled.

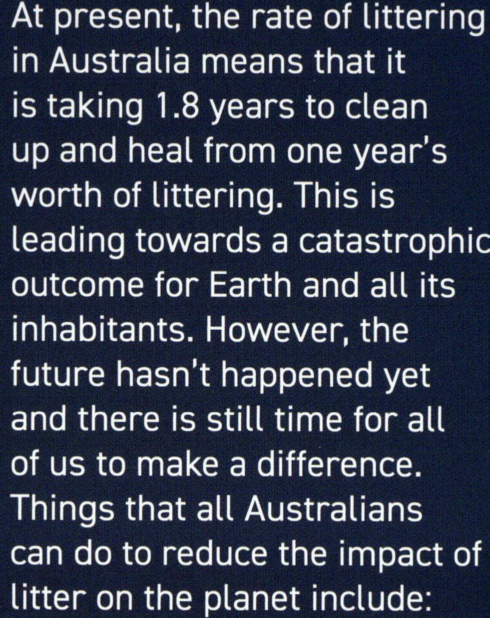

At present, the rate of littering in Australia means that it is taking 1.8 years to clean up and heal from one year's worth of littering. This is leading towards a catastrophic outcome for Earth and all its inhabitants. However, the future hasn't happened yet and there is still time for all of us to make a difference. Things that all Australians can do to reduce the impact of litter on the planet include:

- Buying products that are made to last
- Buying clothing and furniture from stores that encourage goods to be returned to the store at the end of their life
- Buying recycled products to improve the demand for their manufacture
- Avoiding single-use items such as plastic bags, straws and most food packaging
- Repairing broken items instead of replacing them with new ones
- Learning how to recycle properly
- Considering buying second-hand products before buying anything new
- Planning meals to reduce food waste – a major contributor to greenhouse gas emissions
- If you have a backyard, consider keeping chickens, a worm farm and starting a compost bin

GLOSSARY

biodegradable capable of being decomposed by bacteria or other living organisms

climate change process by which the overall climate varies between one temperature and a new average temperature

composting mixing food scraps with soil so that they can break down to produce nutrient-rich soil

drought period of little or no rainfall

entrepreneur person who sets up a business

exoskeleton external skeleton that supports and protects an animal's body, like a shell

global warming increase in the overall climate of the planet caused by the release of greenhouse gases into the atmosphere

greenhouse gases invisible gases in the atmosphere that trap the heat from the Sun

landfill large pit in the ground where waste is buried and left to decompose

litter food waste, packaging and other trash left in public places

monsoon very heavy rainfall

pollution the introduction of harmful materials into the environment

recycle process waste material so that it can be used again

volunteer person who freely offers their services without asking for payment

INDEX